Heal The Planet, Heal Your Soul

Awaken Through Veganism

Renee Raia

Heal the Planet, Heal Your Soul
Renee Raia

Copyright © 2017 Renee Raia

Cover design by Jill and Phil Pottle
ForeverPhotographyNYC.com

This book is offered for educational and informational purposes only and should not be used as a re-placement for the medical advice of your health care provider. All efforts have been made to ensure the accuracy of the information as of the date published. The author and publisher disclaim responsibility for any adverse effects arising from the use or application of the information contained herein.

This book is dedicated to Jack for giving me a beautiful earth experience and to Joe for showing me Heaven is real.

Table of Contents

About the Author

Renee Raia is the author of this book. She is a Reiki attuned, awakened soul who is highly empathetic to planetary and humanitarian concerns. After having a spiritual awakening, she felt guided within her soul to step into divine service. Learning about energy through shamans combined with an awakening resulted in a clear understanding of energy and the divine soul. She lives a very clean lifestyle to maintain a high vibration by engaging in a vegan lifestyle, practicing yoga and daily meditation. Renee finds it so rewarding to help people find their inner light through unconditional divine love. She is a vegan cook that provides food for spiritual communities, some of which she leads in meditation. Renee finds much joy in helping others find their way to a peaceful existence.

Renee has great compassion for all people, regardless of their diet, and writes this book to offer awareness to the many benefits, some of which may not be obvious, of a vegan diet for people and the planet.

She was just like most Americans, eating a Standard American Diet (SAD), until at age 20 when she made the transition to a vegetarian diet for health reasons. After 13 years of a vegetarian diet, she learned about how dairy caused health problems and the inhumane way conventional dairy cows are treated, and so, she adopted a vegan diet. After being vegan for eight years, she was surprised that the diet had a transformative impact beyond her physical body. She discovered the high vibration food had a spiritual impact and had awakened her soul.

Contact Renee if you are interested in learning more about her upcoming unique workshops combining veganism, meditation, cooking, healing and spirituality.

Email: VeganbyRenee@gmail.com
Website: VeganbyRenee.com
Instagram: Vegan_by_Renee
Facebook: Angel Ren

Introduction

It is my wish that this book will help many to participate in unity consciousness. If we can understand the sacred connection of energy in which we all share, healing and purification on all levels are possible. Each and every one of us is a creation of divine energy, even if we don't feel that sacred connection at all times. This book will help the reader understand how food and energy relate to every aspect of our existence. Discover how your food choices can have an energetic effect on our ecosystems, which physically and spiritually sustain us. Eating food that is photosynthesized directly by the sun positively assists mother earth and all who inhabit her in their healing process. Considering that energy is the language of the universe and cannot be destroyed, we can then understand our existence through a spiritual lens. We can then understand what happens to the energy of our loved ones who pass on. Healing can take place when we understand our soul is made of energy that is eternal, and departed loved ones exist in another dimension. Here you will discover some of the ways loved ones communicate with us when they return to source. It is my sacred wish for my fellow human beings to heal through this knowledge and make a positive contribution to the miraculous, energetic web of life.

Chapter 1:
The Positive Impacts of Veganism

We live on a planet made of energy. The earth itself can be considered a massive ecosystem. Our ecosystems are energetically and divinely designed to keep Mother Earth in balance. As such, a clean environment ensures the protection of biodiversity and ecosystems, upon which all life on earth depends. An unbalanced ecosystem leads to death of certain animals and plants, unsafe drinking water, air pollution, climate change, new diseases, and degradation of human health. We can certainly agree that none of us truly want human activity to place chronic stress on this ecosystem.

The forest is one of the world's largest eco-systems; it consists of micro-organisms, plants, and animals that help keep everything in balance, or homeostasis. A healthy forest provides us with clean air, purifies our rain, and allows for the growth of medicinal plants, seeds, nuts, syrups and saps, etc. Additionally, it secures employment for those in the business of timber harvesting, which provides material for housing, furniture, and much more. Humans benefit tremendously from a healthy forest. Not only do large forests influence regional weather patterns by promoting rainfall, they also purify the water and air we require to survive. The water that gets past the majestic tree roots trickle down into the aquifers that clean toxic water. Trees are necessary to purify the acid rain that results from air pollution. Conversely, the animal waste from factory farming pollutes our air, rivers, and streams. As we continue clearing away our natural filtration system by releasing these feces, antibiotics, and parasites, we continue to cripple our collective ecosystem. Acid rain is dangerous to our forests, as it weakens the tree leaves, which limits the nutrients available to them. Therefore, air pollution that causes acid rain is not conducive to a healthy forest, and an unhealthy forest is not conducive to healthy lives for humans or animals that share this planet. There are so many benefits to a healthy forest, it behooves us to protect and honor them.

Sadly, the current state of industry and human-led destruction includes the excessive clearing of these forests, known as deforestation, for the purpose of factory-farming animals. Considering the forests offer us the very things we need to live, it is in our greatest interests to be their safe keepers. The overconsumption of mass-produced meat is a major contributing factor in the earth's pollution, and as mentioned, it demolishes the natural filtration systems we rely on for a healthy earth. This unnatural method of mass-producing meat is hurting our environment, and the only one's truly benefitting are companies in the form of enormous financial gains. The forests are an important lifeline for humanity.

Protecting the air ecosystem is also of vital importance. Given the choice, I am certain we would all choose to breathe fresh air. As an example, pig factories are major contributors to air pollution. An average pig factory generates the same amount of waste as a city populated with approximately 12,000 people! The manure and urine are stored in huge manmade waste lagoons, also known as earth basins. These basins have been the cheapest method of "treating waste," but they are responsible for air pollution that causes breathing problems, unfavorable stench, and depressed property values. Besides these waste lagoons contributing to air pollution, the greenhouse gasses produced by cattle farming are also major contributors to poor air quality. Climate change, headaches, nausea, respiratory disease, and allergies are quantifiable side effects of methane emissions.

Do you see how raping the land to mass produce meat is creating an imbalance in our air and forest ecosystems? We have to become aware of the impact factory farming has on our planet. Polluting the air and destroying the forest shows blatant disregard for our planet. As a result of the ongoing genocide of animals, the planet is suffering catastrophically.

Yes, it is true that Native Americans consumed meat, but they also held reverence for the land and all creatures that inhabited the earth. There was a sacred connection between all living beings, and there was an understanding to the rhythm of nature. These tribal men and women understood what impact we have on our Mother Earth.

Our oceans are another important ecosystem. When we don't disturb the balance of natural plants, animals, and other components, the marine ecosystem remains in balance. We can observe the natural cycle of each species and understand the relationship between them. It is only man-made disturbances that truly disrupt the balance of the ecosystem. For example, bottom trawling is a dangerous method of commercial fishing. Large nets are dragged across the ocean floor in an attempt to catch those fish that remain near the bottom of the ocean, and as a result, these practices destroy centuries-old sea coral and everything else in their path. This method of fishing kills dolphins, birds, sea lions, and other "bycatch" animals. Trawling disturbs our finely balanced and very complex systems.

Sometimes, changing one part of an ecosystem can cause the whole system to undergo changes. No matter the size of the individual components, these systems are symbiotic communities. The reefs support an enormous amount of life and diversity, and they are vitally important nurseries for young fish. We are now discovering that reefs could also be important source of medicine to treat human diseases.

The ongoing over consumption and mass production of animals for food is a major contributing factor in the pollution and destructive imbalance of our planet. It would be greatly beneficial for the health of planet, and thus for us as well, to forage food without entirely raping the land and oceans. In our day-to-day lives, we may not realize the extent of natural resources we rely on. We rely on petroleum to produce electricity and gasoline. We use rocks and granite for our homes, schools, and other buildings. Our jeans are made of cotton, and the zippers are made of copper and zinc. Eyeglasses and windows are made of quartz, sand, and petroleum.

Even though these are nonrenewable resources, we still have the earth to thank for them. However, these resources are extracted significantly faster than the rate at which they form naturally. Once they are depleted, they are depleted for good. Therefore, we owe it to our planet and ourselves to be mindful of any act that contributes to harming Mother Earth.

"Reduce, reuse, and recycle" has been a popular catch phrase throughout the late 20th and early 21st centuries. As we continue to evolve as humans, and find our happiness within, maybe there will be less need to waste and want. We can make choices that honor our planet. Recycling helps the environment by reducing our need to use natural resources to make new products. We can reuse by donating what we no longer use, and thus reduce consumption. As we honor our planet, we will benefit by living in harmony with her. Clean air, clean water, and pure foods are imperative to our healthy existence. Our mindfulness today will allow future generations to reap the benefits of a healthy planet, and we can make a positive contribution to this beautiful planet just by making a few adjustments to our lifestyles. Here are some helpful hints:

1. Be mindful of where your food comes from. A vegan diet doesn't cause harm to the planet, and it can help eradicate world hunger, as more people can be fed by the crops and land that is used to feed animals raised for consumption. It can also support an organic and healthy environment, shows compassion to our fellow human being, and spares unnecessary torment to animals.

2. Avoid products that are not biodegradable as much as possible. The more synthetic items we use and later "get rid of," the more we have to burn or bury in the earth for disposal. With billions of

people on the planet, it would be beneficial for us to keep this in mind.

3. Composting reduces the amount of solid waste produced and helps your soil remain healthy. There would be less space taken up in landfills if the majority of people were on board with composting.

4. Make your home energy efficient by cleaning filters, turning off lights, using compact fluorescent light bulbs (CFL), and being mindful of running water. When upgrading appliances, look into energy star appliances to ensure you're not using more energy than necessary. This will help you save money as well.

5. Savor the foods of the season. Eating fruits and vegetables in season will reduce your carbon footprint by minimizing the distance the produce has to travel

before it is on your plate. It is also great to support local farms and businesses.

6. Bring your own bag to pack groceries. Plastic does not break down, and large areas of land and ocean are littered with plastics that harm the ecosystem. For example, scientists discovered a gigantic mass of plastic floating in the Pacific Ocean, which is proven to be a huge threat to marine life.

7. Look into non-toxic cleaning products to avoid indoor pollutants.

8. Avoid using disposable water bottles. Each year, 17 million barrels of oil are used in the production of disposable water bottles!

9. Learn about the importance of bees. Bees transfer pollen and seeds from one flow-er to another, fertilizing plants, which in

turn allows them to produce food. This process of cross-pollination helps at least 30% of the world crops and 90% of our wild plants to thrive. Without the bees to spread seeds, many food crops would die off completely. While some plants will self-pollinate, most require the service of the bees. If our wild plants don't thrive, there will be a negative impact on the balance of our ecosystem and our food supply. Planting flowers, such as Blackeyed Susans, purple coneflowers, and elder flowers, just to name a few, will help bolster the bee population. It is also helpful to use chemical-free lawn care products.

When we are in nature that is undisturbed, perhaps on a pristine beach, a forest, or a meadow, we can appreciate the beauty of our planet. Time spent in undisturbed nature strengthens the immune system, fills our lungs with clean air, increases our energy, improves our moods, and so much more. The earth offers so much to us, and it is our duty and obligation to make choices that will help sustain her. It is beneficial to the planet to refrain from having excessive material goods, just as it is a benefit to your soul to find true happiness from within. You will find that you can do with less. Replace an empty lifestyle of hollow purchases with a fulfilling nourishing of your soul. Time and energy are much more valuable than material possessions. When you depart into the spirit world and reach a clear level of consciousness, you will have great satisfaction knowing you did not abuse your mother earth. Our sacred earth, which is over 400 billion years old, sustains us during our incarnation and our pilgrimage. Our search for spiritual peace and wellness is fulfilled as we honor each other and the planet. We must learn to live in a way that honors mother earth so we can live in harmony with her.

Chapter 2:
Veganism and Our Bodies

In 1944, Donald Watson coined the phrase "vegan," but there is evidence of people choosing to avoid animal consumption as far back as 2,000-plus years ago. Food is categorized as being acidic, neutral, or alkaline. A highly alkaline diet is better for your health, and the regulation of the acid-alkaline balance within our bodies is imperative to remaining healthy. If our body is too acidic, it is difficult for enzymes to function properly, which then leads to sickness. An example of acidic forming foods would be meat, dairy, sugar, breads, caffeinated drinks, sweeteners, alcohol, rice, and some nuts. An example of alkalizing foods would be most fruits, vegetables, sprouted beans, and coconuts. Neutral foods include oils and raw milk, which have neither an alkaline nor acidic effect on the body when consumed.

As we learned in the previous chapter, incorporating more plant foods into our diets has a positive impact on the environment. To add to those benefits, let's explore how a vegan and alkaline-rich diet supports great health in the human body. The pH (potential hydrogen) of our body needs to remain in a careful balance for the best possible health. One of the benefits of an alkaline-rich environment within our bodies is that cancer cannot thrive. Eating plenty of vegetables and fruits help keep our pH balanced, and it provides us with the antioxidants needed to counteract the damaging effects of free radicals.

A free radical is a molecule that is missing an electron in their outer shell. To fill in the outer shell, electrons are stolen from the body's cellular structure, which may result in damaged

DNA and cell membranes. When your cells are damaged, you are vulnerable to disease and accelerated aging. An alkaline-rich diet will certainly put the odds for great health in your favor. The human body produces free radicals when converting food to energy. Antioxidants counteract the damaging effects of free radicals by neutralizing and removing them from the bloodstream. If we do not have antioxidants to keep our cells healthy, toxic compounds that are formed may begin a chain reaction of oxidative stress. Eating a mostly acidic diet makes your body work harder to maintain a neutral, alkaline zone. Your body must compensate for high intake of acid forming foods by taking calcium from your bones. This increases your chance of getting osteoporosis. Organs such as the liver and pancreas produce alkaline enzymes to reduce excess acidity, but even with these alkalizing mechanisms at work, there are still times when pH levels drop below the required 7.38 pH. When this occurs, the body begins to break down bone and muscle tissue for their alkalizing ammonia carbonates and phosphates. Studies show an acid diet is a contributing factor in obesity, diabetes, cardiovascular disease, inflammation, colon cancer, high cholesterol, and more. Why would we want to contribute to the aging process of our body by forcing it to work harder?

Considering that fats are difficult for the body to digest, it is healthier to balance your diet in that aspect as well. When fat moves into your small intestines, the gallbladder releases bile to help break them down into smaller particles for absorption into the bloodstream. The liver produces the bile, and the gallbladder holds it until it is required for digestion. Approximately 85% of bile is made from water, making proper hydration necessary for healthy body function. A clean, balanced diet, fresh water, and clean air help keep our cells clear and healthy. Alkalizing foods help protect healthy cells, balance essential mineral levels, prevent plaque formation in blood vessels, stop calcium from accumulating in urine, prevent kidney stones, and much more.

Enjoy this fun but far from comprehensive list of plant foods that are healing, high vibration and delicious!

Food	Health Benefits
Apples	Help reduce the risk of developing cancer, diabetes, and heart disease.
Bananas	Help maintain strong, flexible blood vessels and possess anti-oxidants, anti-inflammatory, and anti-cancer properties.
Cinnamon	Anti-carcinogenic, anti-bacterial, and anti-viral properties.

Food	Health Benefits
Dill Weed	Good source of calcium, manganese, and iron. It is an antioxidant food with anti-inflammatory properties as well.
Edamame	Improves bone and cardiovascular health, builds a stronger immune system.
Fennel	Contains fiber, potassium, folate, vitamins C and B6.
Garlic	Has potent medicinal properties, vitamins, and manganese. Also boosts the function of the immune system, reduces blood pressure, and helps detoxify heavy metals in the body.

Food	Health Benefits
Honeydew	Contains vitamin C and copper, which aids in tissue repair and helps maintain healthy blood pressure levels.
Iceberg lettuce	Contains vitamin K, which supports skeletal health, and vitamin A, which supports the health of your eyes, skin, and blood.
Jalapeno peppers	Rich source of vitamin C, which prevents damage from free radicals, and a great source of vitamin A, which supports the health of your eyes, skin, and blood.
Kale	Great source of vitamins K, C, B6, manganese, calcium, copper, and potassium. It is one of the most nutrient-dense foods on the planet.

Food	Health Benefits
Leeks	Have many health benefits, such as beta-carotene, vitamins C and E, and many minerals, which all works together to strengthen the immune system and so much more.
Macadamia nuts	Rich source of vitamin A, iron, protein, folates, amino acids, potassium, magnesium, and much more.
Nectarines	Good source of beta-carotene, vitamins A and C, fiber, and potassium.
Oranges	Provide a range of vitamins and minerals as well as having anti-inflammatory properties. They are also known to be strong antioxidants.

Food	Health Benefits
Parsley	Packed with calcium, iron, folate, vitamins K and C, and possesses anti-inflammatory properties and much more.
Radishes	Have folate, fiber, riboflavin, potassium, copper, vitamin B6, calcium, magnesium, and fiber.
Spinach	Full of minerals, high nutritional value in antioxidants, many vitamins, iron, magnesium, calcium, and much more.

Food	Health Benefits
Turnips	These belong to the cruciferous family and contain high levels of antioxidants and phytochemicals, which help to reduce the risk of cancer. They possess great anti-inflammatory properties as a result of being packed with vitamin K. They support bone and lung health, aid in digestion, strengthen the immune system, and help to prevent body odor.
Upland cress or watercress	An herb that is indigenous to Europe and resembles curled parsley, it has a delightful zesty flavor and is an excellent source of several nutrients, vitamins, minerals, protein, and folate.

Food	Health Benefits
Vanilla bean	Contains magnesium, potassium, calcium, and manganese. Vanilla bean is also an aphrodisiac, which enhances hormones in the body associated with feeling love and happiness.
Watermelon	Beneficial in reducing inflammation and rich in antioxidants, which neutralize free radicals.
Xinomavro grapes or any red grapes	Originated in Greece and are commonly used to make wine. They contain powerful antioxidants that may slow or prevent many types of cancer, and they support cardiovascular health.

Food	Health Benefits
Yams	Good source of vitamin C, which supports wound healing, anti-aging, and immune functions. Yams also provide us with a good amount of fiber, potassium, and metabolic B vitamins.
Zucchini	Contains vitamin A, magnesium, potassium, copper, omega 3 fatty acids, zinc, protein, and B vitamins.

Mother Earth also blesses us with medicinal plants. For example, the chamomile plant is used to treat problems within the digestive system, bronchitis, cough, and fever. The essential oils taken from the tea tree shrub is a popular antiseptic used for stings, burns wounds, and other skin conditions. Organic plants and food from the earth fully sustain us. Because "we are what we eat," we can make the choice to eat nutrient rich food and experience great vibrant health and a life with less sickness.

Chapter 3:
Spiritual Purification

There are many ways to access our spiritual self. First, we have to know what we are looking to experience. Being spiritual is having a sacred, divine, and holy understanding that we exist as an eternal energy or soul that cannot be destroyed. Realization of soul and self can happen when we lift our consciousness into the formless invisible field of energy, into an infinite dimension. This existence is beyond all limitations and time. This awareness allows us to experience light and love, which is the highest vibration there is to experience. This vibration transcends the belief of the ego and lifts us to a higher state of consciousness – something more than your physical reality and dimension. Knowing your true soul essence is knowing your spiritual self. Regardless of your faith or religion, the fact is that we exist and come from the same source of energy. I refer to this source of energy as God, source, heaven, or the divine. It is a place where all energy exists, including angels, saints, departed loved ones, spirit guides, and ascended masters. When the physical body dies, our souls return to that same field of energy – a field where we aren't separated like some of us feel on the physical planes. Under the layers of human emotion and ego is a pure energy and consciousness comprised of eternal love and light.

A diet rich in fruits and vegetables is one of the strongest means of spiritual purification. Diet and consciousness are interrelated, and purity of diet is an effective aid to clarify consciousness. The food we eat determines the quality and condition of all levels of our being. Plant foods are filled with prana, a vital life force energy. When this prana is consumed, we feel more energized, aware, and pure. Clean eating results in clear thinking. Eating prana food helps raise our vibration, which is simply a method to describe our overall state of wellbeing.

We are comprised of physical and spiritual levels of energy. Everything on earth is made of energy vibrating at different frequencies. Some vibrations are high, and some vibrations are low. Lower vibrations are negative emotions, poor health, lack of spiritual awareness, and disempowering thoughts. Higher vibrations are empowering thoughts, great health, and strong spiritual awareness. Energetically speaking, like attracts like, and your vibe attracts people and circumstances to you. By the law of attraction, you attract the vibration that you emit. Eating for your vibration will enhance your joy and attract more positive experiences and people to you.

Although this may all seem very mystical, what we eat directly translates to our spiritual wellness. It is helpful to have a clean and healthy vessel that houses your spiritual temple. For us to raise ourselves into higher consciousness, we must purify our thoughts and our food. Besides an energy rich diet raising your spiritual vibration, your level of physical energy will also increase. Being mindful of our thoughts and our food choices is directly related to our wellness and states of mind. We incarnate with a divine plan and evolve to the best completion of our souls' mission. A higher level of vibration and awareness will help clarify your individual journey and spiritual growth.

We incarnate to heal, learn, evolve, and ultimately reach enlightenment. The level of consciousness we are experiencing determines how close or far we are from enlightenment. There is no right or wrong, just a simple observation of how far along we or others are on their path. When negative emotions come up, they are a gift for your soul. They are simply showing you parts of yourself that haven't yet healed. They come up to be purified and released, allowing the true nature of your soul to emerge. Your soul doesn't need to carry what comes up for healing and can be released from your force field. Thank the lessons and release them. As we heal, purify, and shed our pain, we will ultimately reach enlightenment. That is the purpose and true nature of the soul.

There isn't any judgement by human standards in which this enlightenment is achieved. It is a process of growth and evolving for the soul. Divine timing, destiny, and free will are running the show. If our free will is not aligned with our soul plan, we will feel very uncomfortable. When a flower is ready to bloom, it must bloom. There is no question why people trying to spiritually purify partake in prana-rich foods.

Being spiritual is also being compassionate and expressing it through non-violence toward all sentient beings. As we evolve on our spiritual journey, and experience higher levels of consciousness, we simply won't be able to support any violent actions. Society's moral principles must come under serious scrutiny for those who support factory farming. In our capitalist society, animals have become objects for consumption and a commodity for profits. There is very little consideration for the suffering they endure. Slaughterhouses are guarded like military institutions, and the public isn't always aware that many animals are unconscious during transport to the slaughterhouses and live a very painful existence. It is honestly too gruesome and painful for me to stain the pages of this book with the dreadful details of the imprisoned, mutilated, and violently killed animals.

Consuming meat from an animal that is pumped full of vaccines, antibiotics, and growth hormones, and had a painful existence, will not support spiritual or physical health. The adrenaline, stress, and torture endured are stored in the animal's meat, and these negative energies are passed along to the person consuming it. Eating energy food fully supports the spiritual purification process.

Chapter 4:
This Energetic Web of Life

We are so much more than our limited, physical selves; we are an undying infinite energy. When you contemplate the magical energy of the universe, and understand your connection to it, you will notice the synchronicities and miracles taking place. Some people call them coincidences, but they are actually signs from the universe pulling you forward on the unique path your life takes. Through meditation and prayer, we are able to experience the connection to our soul by lifting our consciousness to a higher state of awareness; we are able to transcend our limited human beliefs, pain, and emotions. When we align with the pure essence of our being, we reach new levels of enlightenment and feel the divine nature of our soul. It can be a challenge to stay in this energetic frequency for long periods of time, but we can always come back to this state of awareness.

Of course, we do exist in a human body; we are here to learn. As more people awaken their spiritual nature, it will become easier for the collective to maintain a higher vibration, and there will be less negativity to transmute. When we recognize the truth of our energetic existence, we can clear and heal any negative beliefs that we have been conditioned and programmed to believe. Our soul is made of energy, and energy is the language of the universe. You can sense the "vibe," the energetic vibration of those around you without any words uttered. It is not always realized that the law of attraction is referring to your vibrational frequency that draws people and circumstances towards you.

The soul will emit a frequency that offers you the lesson you must learn, and it will repeat this frequency until the lesson is learned. At times, certain lessons can feel like a punishment, but it is actually a gift of learning for your soul. We certainly don't want to stay in a loop of attracting negativity over and over. As the soul evolves toward enlightenment, all human characteristics are purified. If your soul has to learn forgiveness, see the person triggering you in their divine light, and purify yourself by forgiving them. It is best to view the lesson from a higher, healing perspective and allow your soul to move forward towards enlightenment. If wounds come up to be healed, it is so you can clear the negativity and move into a state of increased joy. The evolution of your soul is always working toward realization, completion, and enlightenment. Every person and situation in your life is divinely placed there for the sake of your learning. Your light body or soul will forever exist and the temporary experiences we have while in our physical body are experienced to help us move toward enlightenment.

Many times, we go through life forgetting our divinity. We all come from the same cosmic web of energy, but we sometimes realize that at different times during our incarnation. It is a gift to become awakened while alive in the human body. Using the analogy of the layers within an onion, we are all pure, divine light at the very center. What needs to be peeled away to reach that light will determine how many layers we have to work through. There is no judgement towards where a person stands in their evolution, but a simple, peaceful, and non-reactive acknowledgement and observation of what can be done to further their enlightenment. We do not live in a material universe, but in one of energy. We can project our energy by focusing our attention in the desired direction.

The human mind mirrors a universe that mirrors the human mind. Our words, actions, and thoughts are energy creating our reality. In the Aramaic language, "Abra qe dabra," translates to, "I will create as I speak." Where attention goes, energy flows. The more connected to the source of energy in which we come from, the more alive and energized we feel. When we feel cut off from a greater source of energy, we tend to try and gain it from another person. Doing so will not lead us to feeling inner peace, though. When we feel our connection to self and source, we can experience divine energy within and understand a true sense of wholeness. If human beings can unite in this dimension of existence, and lift their awareness to a higher state of consciousness, we will all benefit. Because we are connected through the mass consciousness, it benefits us all every time an enlightened person stays true to their divine nature and sends out a frequency of love. As we evolve, we become more aware that all of humanity comes from the same source of energy. That source is not divided by politics, countries, religion, or any other manmade division. That source is simply another dimension in which we exist.

Thanks to celestial and astrological knowledge, the Mayans and other past civilizations were able to see into humanity's future. They foretold the transformation of unity consciousness, a new paradigm of existence. The year 2012 was the beginning of global awakening, kick-started by cosmic waves of higher frequencies. We are all being pulled forward to knock down the illusionary walls of separation. More and more people are realizing the connection we have to one another and the vast energy field we call source or heaven.

Astrological weather ties into our existence. Roughly speaking, every 2,150 years, the sun's position moves in front of a new zodiac constellation. The Age of Aquarius began when we moved out of the age of Pisces. Under the influence of Pisces, humanity was dominated by hierarchy and power, and people attached themselves to a political ideology, a charismatic leader, or only had tolerance for their religion. At this time, unity consciousness was not practiced. These traits have been the foundation for the human consciousness for many years. There was a limited awareness without introspection regarding humanity being connected through the divine energy that we share. There wasn't much room for contemplation, just following what was taught without any independent thinking. As we shifted into the Age of Aquarius, humanity started to veer toward self-awareness, transformation, growth, oneness, and our own evolution. When we realize we share an energetic connection with all of humanity, the planet, and beyond, perhaps we won't feel a need to dominate another being for their energy. We can center ourselves to feel our very own connection to the divine source of energy in which we come from. It is no longer serving humanity to come from a place of fear and separation.

The ancient and indigenous cultures had prophecies of this new cycle. We simply cannot exist peacefully on this planet without realizing we are all in this together. Despite what it may seem like on earth, in the heavenly realms, we only share love. In 1967, a group called the Fifth Dimension wrote a smash hit about the Age of Aquarius. The opening lines are, "When the moon is in the seventh house, and Jupiter aligns with Mars, then peace will guide the planets and love will steer the stars. This is the dawning of the Age of Aquarius." As we evolve in consciousness, we can actually appreciate the person in our life that triggers us; they are helping us learn our soul's lessons. Each person we meet is divinely placed in our lives. Having love and compassion for self and others is a high level of spiritual intelligence. The person who needs our forgiveness is actually helping us with our spiritual ascension. Our energetic frequency is actually helping us "walk each other home" An enlightened being gets there by purifying, which happens when we alchemize the human condition and see only from a divine perspective. If we view our relationships through a spiritual lens, we can see where compassion is needed and what lessons need to be learned.

Regardless of what our relationships look like from a human perspective, in the heavenly realms we agreed before incarnating to have these experiences. We agreed to play certain roles for the growth of our soul. There are many ways to nourish your soul and experience your divine essence. Meditation is a great way to enter a trance-like state and lift your consciousness. The word trance can be better described as a half-conscious state characterized by an absence of response to external stimuli. We have the opportunity to reconnect with ourselves during meditation to feel a true sense of peace and anchor into the connection we have with the divine. When life gets too busy and noisy, it is possible to feel disconnected from source although it is impossible to sever our energetic tie to the field of energy from which we come. Any time we feel divine love, which is the very nature of our soul, we are uplifted to a magical state of love, safety, bliss, and joy.

Manifestations are possible when your vibration is high and you trust in the intelligence of the universe. Detachment from outcomes derive from trusting the intelligence of the universe and your connection to it. A lower vibration of fear is not helpful and is not in alignment with trust and faith. When we are on our path, the universe will unveil synchronicity that will continue guiding us, and thus, life will flow easily. The natural evolution of the soul is to come into full realization and acceptance of self, and know we are eternal energy of light made of pure love. When you reach this state, you will see through the human illusions, and exist in a state of love, non-attachment, light, and compassion.

Chapter 5:
Higher Levels of Consciousness

Naturally, many people wonder about existence on the spiritual planes. At a certain point in our evolution, we may ask:

"What happens to our loved ones when they return to source?"

"Is it possible to connect with them when they are no longer with us physically?"

"Will they send me a sign?"

It is fascinating to experience a "god wink" or hear of an experience of communication with a deceased loved one. We are all born with a thin veil between us and the heavenly realms. As life progresses, the noise and distractions of life sometimes interfere with us feeling our heavenly connections. Upon departing into the spirit world, we tend to straddle both worlds, and the veil becomes thin yet again. I have been humbly grateful to observe a loved one, who was within a week of going back to source, connecting with her loved ones who had already passed. In her last days, she said, "I was just with my mother and grandmother, and now I am back here."

In the course of our busy lives, it is very easy to miss these divine signs unless we truly quiet the mind and tune into a higher awareness and frequency. I have been blessed to awaken and experience a full-blown spiritual and kundalini awakening. The awakening of kundalini energy has nothing to do with culture or religion, although it is described in yoga texts. It is the natural evolution of the human being to awaken to higher levels of consciousness to experience soul realization. Awakenings and coming into full self-realization is a blessing, although there can be an intense period of purification as the soul becomes realized. Events that are destined to take place on the physical realms are divinely influenced and guided. At the time of this awakening, I experienced a consciousness of pure love and light. Food and sleep didn't feel like necessities, as I was living in spirit. There was a true detachment from anything human.

During this time, I've experienced a full connection to the divine, which was a feeling far greater than any human experience. Divine love is so much more blissful than romantic or human love. Whatever emotions we experience as humans, such as fear worry, hurt, etc., do not exist in that dimension. Material possessions do not matter at all at that level of awareness. During that heavenly experience, I felt the presence of a woman who I have never met, but left a son behind after she and her husband passed away. It felt as if her soul merged with mine, and I experienced the love she had for her son. This connection was experienced at the highest level of consciousness imaginable, which one can describe as heaven. I instinctively and intuitively knew to care for her child on the physical realm as she guided me from the spiritual realm. At this time, my veil was thin, as I straddled both physical and spiritual realities.

After being awakened to a much higher level of consciousness, the true essence of the soul becomes realized. Besides experiencing a feeling of true divinity flowing through my entire being, that level of vibration allowed the channels of communication to remain open for my soul to receive divine guidance. At this time, I experienced firsthand that when our loved ones pass away, they continue to exist and are able to send messages and communicate with us if it is God's will. As we awaken to the spiritual realms, we become very familiar with another dimension of our existence. The human experience of the calling was one of loss, grief, worry, confusion, and an overwhelming feeling of responsibility. The spiritual aspect of the calling was one of miracles, love, faith, and heaven. It was a blessing to experience the human reality and simultaneously the intangible world of energy. Even though the mother needing my help departed this world, and her soul became limitless and free, the love she has for her son is undying. My soul accepted this great honor to be of divine service. We don't always understand why things happen on the physical planes, but rest assured there is a divine purpose. If we don't know what our life purpose is during our incarnation, we will certainly see it clearly when we return to source.

What if this painful experience led me to know there is a divine? Would we seek or experience the light if there were no contrast? I stayed tuned into a frequency of divine love for the duration of the calling. Deceased loved ones reach out to us in many ways. Besides messages coming through our senses, they can be sent as songs, numbers, animal totems, feathers, coins, electrical devices, dreams, tingling, heat on the body, and messages through people.

Here is a list of how our senses are used for divine communication.

Sense	Explanation
Clairaudience	Clear hearing and the ability to hear sounds or voices that are not audible to the normal ear.
Clairolfaction	Being able to smell a scent or energy where no one else can. It is having a psychic nose.
Clairvoyant	Clear seeing. It is seeing through your third eye or your mind's eye. It can appear as a very clear image.
Clairgustance	Clear tasting. An example would be suddenly having the taste of a deceased loved one's favorite food in your mouth when their spirit is with you.

Sense	Explanation
Claircognizance	The intuitive ability to know. This is the most doubted of these abilities because it is hard to discern what is thought and what comes from the spirit.
Clairsentience	Clear sensing. It is the ability to feel the present, past, and future, physical and emotional state of others.

Losing a loved one can leave us feeling empty, full of grief, angry, and lifeless. It is in those times that we cherish a message from them letting us know their soul is free and they are no longer bound by time or any human restrictions. When our loved ones return to source, they are pure energy and are able to channel their energy into an animal for a brief period of time to bring us a sign that their spirit lives on. They want us to be free of the pain we carry from losing them. During the divine calling, there were many times that, from a human perspective, there seemed to be no hope and the situation was dire. It was in these times, I would lift my consciousness to one of full faith and trust, and I was able to tune into a higher frequency to receive the signs from the universe and loved ones in spirit. At this time of awakening, communication from higher realms came in many ways, as I was completely tuned into the energy field. When I asked for answers and help, I tuned into the present moment, had full trust, and asked for a sign. I simply observed without overthinking anything. There were plenty of times during the calling where panic could have easily set in, but one particular time, the universe was kind enough to show me a praying mantis on my kitchen window as I asked for help. The totem for when you see a praying mantis is stillness and patience.

As another example of animal communication, there was a time where my emotions were running high due to the challenges I faced, but outside, there came two ducks on my front lawn. This may seem unsurprising, but it is a very unlikely occurrence where I live. The totem for ducks is to check your emotions. This reminder and support from the spirit let me know to trust and not let my emotions get the best of me. I learned to trust the scary moments, ask for guidance, and keep the faith. Even when the boy almost died, or when the heating system in his house went and I had no idea how I was coming up with the money needed to get him a new system. Although these challenging situations were presented to me for years, it was an opportunity for me to have reinforcement from the heavenly realms, signs and encouragement to keep going and have faith that it will all work out. And it always did.

I often pondered if one person's suffering lighted the way for others. Did the person needing my help propel my soul into full awareness of all that is? Do our painful experiences prepare us to be of divine service? How many times do you see people suffer and later become advocates for their cause? I have learned that pain is a form of purification of the soul. This experience gave me the opportunity to know our loved ones are always around, and if we tune in, we are able to see the signs and know they are with us. I also learned not to puncture my wholeness with fear-based consciousness. It is such a gift to catch a glimpse of the divine. Shamans and other healers often alter their state of consciousness to fully tap into this field of energy. They do so for healing purposes. There is a divine answer for every human experience we have. Every emotion we have ever felt has been experienced by people since the beginning of humanity. Not a single thought or emotion is uniquely yours.

Regardless of what it seems like in the human dimension, we are lovingly connected to one another. I am eternally grateful for the opportunity I had to serve. As a result of the most heartbreaking tragedy, I awakened to the essence of my soul. Our deceased loved ones are a thought away and reside in a place where time does not exist.

I truly hope and pray this chapter offers some hope and understanding from a spiritual perspective, and supports humanity to be in full alignment with their divine soul. All is love and love is eternal.

Chapter 6:
Meditation

There are many benefits to meditation. Through meditation, we are able to put our mind at ease, regulate emotions, improve concentration, feel our connection to the divine, increase our happiness, reduce stress, slow aging, clear energy blocks, raise our vibration, and more. Some people use essential oils, sound healing with singing bowls and tuning forks, reiki healing, or prayer as other methods of healing. Whichever method resonates with us for healing, divine energy is what we are tuning into and becoming one with.

Monitor your thoughts for the sake of your inner peace. They are creating your reality. Also, refrain from judgement toward yourself and others. Never allow fear-based consciousness to puncture your wholeness.

The breath is a powerful tool. If you are experiencing dense negative energy and cannot step away from it, deeply inhale what you are feeling, and as you exhale, release it to the stars to be purified by the divine. Energetically rid the negative sensation from your being. I learned that very simple yet effective technique from a Shaman. You can also inhale a positive sensation, and when you exhale, you'll be sending it throughout your entire being. These techniques also allow a healthy connection to be made in your brain to support healthy thought patterns.

It is a great honor to lead people to their inner peace by offering a sacred space and meditation. Before meditation, you might want to consider clearing the space by burning white sage, opening a window, and setting the intention of "washing off" the outside world. The Latin word for sage, Salvia, stems from the word "to heal." After the sage is lit, blow out the fire and wave the smoke around the space, clearing away any negative energy. It is the intention set that makes the ritual work. It is also common to light a candle or incense in preparation for meditation. Traditionally, music wasn't played during meditation, but today it seems more common. An example of meditation music is "Healing" by Anugama, or 528-hertz music. Participants would dress in loose fitting clothes and sit comfortably in a circle. Here is just an example of a simple meditation that you can use for yourself or willing participants. If you are going to lead a meditation, use a gentle voice and slowly read the meditation that follows:

Close your eyes and begin to deepen your breath. Deeply inhale through your nose and completely exhale. Deepen your breathing and quiet your mind. Take another deep breath, and as you exhale, release any tension. Let go of any thoughts, and feel your body become relaxed. Feel the stillness of this moment. As you let go of any concerns, observe the rise and fall of your chest with every breath. Allow yourself to slip into a field of pure consciousness. The light coming from your heart space expands with each breath. Through your breath, feel your soul being pure without any attachments. For some, realization of their spiritual self has not yet dawned upon their consciousness. Let there be no judgement or frustration, just love and acceptance. In divine time, every soul will become fully aware and realized. May you always feel aligned with the nature of your divine self and let compassion and love be your guiding light. Slowly bring awareness back to your breath, back to your physical body, and when you are ready, gently open your eyes.

On a path of evolving and healing, meditation is one way to come back to your true nature to experience who you are at the soul level and truly feel your connection to God. In order to experience and maintain our divine peace and connection to self, it is helpful to have a perspective of forgiveness, compassion, and love. Alchemizing and transmuting energy offers positive results, and with practice, it becomes like second nature. Refraining from emotionally charging a negative situation and staying grounded in love is most beneficial for ourselves as well as others. In the higher realms, we only experience love for one another. After all, every person we meet has made a soul contract with us before we incarnated for the sake of learning.

Staying connected to source also helps us from being pulled off track. It is helpful to create an altar in your home as a reminder to take the time to meditate, pray, and feel your connection to the divine. Some people place candles, crystals, or a symbol of the deity you feel connected to on the altar. It is also helpful to take the time for a salt bath, a walk in nature or by the ocean, to listen to music, practice yoga, visit an Ashram, take a course to enhance your hobby, dance, write, find your creative outlet, or serve humanity. This will result in a positive experience that contributes to inner peace.

All of our life lessons and karmic experiences will ultimately lead us back to the same energetic source. Self-realization is the ultimate state of being, and whether we realize it or not, we are all just walking each other home. Understanding that your thoughts, words, and intentions are all energy, it is helpful to align yourself with what you want to experience. Once you experience the true peace, love, and light of your soul, you will find yourself monitoring your thoughts to maintain a high vibration of love.

Chapter 7:
Recipes for Good Health and Compassion

In order to help the reader transition from the Standard American Diet (SAD) into a compassionate, healthy, delicious, and high-energy diet, I am offering some of my favorite and award winning vegan recipes.

I hope you will enjoy them as much as I do!

Coconut Thai and Butter Bean Stew

Ingredients:
¼ cup shallots finely chopped
1 cup sweet onion finely chopped
2 tablespoons olive oil
3 cups cubed sweet potato
1 tablespoon curry powder
1 teaspoon salt
1 teaspoon pepper
1 13.5-ounce can of reduced fat coconut milk
1 cup fresh chopped cilantro
1 cup butter beans
¼ cup black beans

Directions:
Sauté shallots, onions, and oil in a pot for approximately 5-10 minutes or until cooked. Add the cubed potatoes and herbs. Mix well and add the coconut milk. Put a lid on the pot and cook approximately 15 minutes or until cooked. Shut the flame off, and add beans and cilantro.

Basil Pesto

Ingredients:
4 garlic cloves
2 cups of fresh basil
1 cup of cashews
½ cup extra virgin olive oil

Directions:
Add all ingredients into a food processor. This spread goes very well in a cooked portabella mushrooms and arugula salad sandwich. Pesto also goes well with quinoa, red onions, black olives, and cherry tomatoes.

Sweet Masala Patty

Ingredients:
1 large sweet onion
6 fresh garlic cloves
3 15-ounce cans rinsed chick peas
4 teaspoons curry
1 ½ cup cilantro
1 ½ cups of flour

Directions:
Add ingredients to a food processor, one at a time if needed. When the mixture is combined, form patties. Using vegetable oil, place patties in a skillet, browning on both sides. Serve over sautéed kale.

Mushroom and Cream Cheese Filled Phyllo Dough Cups

Ingredients:
24 ounces Portobello mushrooms
2 sweet onions
4 tablespoons olive oil
8 cloves of finely chopped garlic
¼ cup white wine
⅛ cup vegan butter
1 cup fresh parsley
½ teaspoon salt
½ teaspoon pepper
1 8-ounce tub of vegan cream cheese
Prepared phyllo dough cups

Directions:
Sauté onions in oil. Add chopped mushrooms and cook. When the mushrooms are sufficiently cooked, add wine and let it evaporate and cook off a bit. Add the butter, garlic, salt, pepper, and parsley. Allow the mixture to cool off, then mix in a food processor.

Fill the phyllo cups with mixture and bake for 20 minutes in 325 degrees oven.

Vegan Fennel Sausage

Ingredients:
1 8-ounce package of tempeh
½ teaspoon dried basil
½ teaspoon dried oregano
½ teaspoon garlic powder
½ teaspoon onion powder
1 ½ teaspoons dried fennel
¼ teaspoon dried thyme
¼ teaspoon red pepper flakes
¼ cup flour
¼ cup high quality soy sauce
⅛ cup olive oil
Vegetable oil of your choice for frying

Directions:
Steam the tempeh for 15 minutes and set aside to cool. Add tempeh and all ingredients in a bowl and mix well. Form patties in your desired shape. Fry them in a skillet on both sides until browned on both sides. Serve as breakfast sausage with peppers and

onions or in a calzone with vegan cheese and broccoli.

Mojito Bean and Plantain Salsa

Ingredients:
1 cup sweet white onions, finely chopped
¼ cup olive oil
5 cloves garlic, finely chopped
1 cup red bell pepper, finely chopped
1 jalapeno pepper, finely chopped
1 cup tomatoes, finely chopped
1 teaspoon adobo seasoning
¼ cup fresh cilantro, chopped
¼ cup pink beans
½ sweet plantain, fried in vegetable oil and
   cut into small pieces

Directions:
In a deep skillet, combine olive oil and onions, and cook on a low to medium flame until the onions are translucent, for approximately 10 minutes. Add the garlic and cook for approximately 5 minutes. Stir the mixture occasionally to prevent sticking to the bottom of the skillet. Add peppers and cook for

about 15 minutes. Add tomatoes and cook for 5 minutes. Add adobo and cilantro. Mix well and shut the flame off. Add the beans and plantains. This dish is delicious as it is, served with crackers, stuffing for peppers, or with pasta.

Mock Tuna Salad

Ingredients:
1 15-ounce can of chick peas
5 tablespoons vegan mayonnaise
3 tablespoons mustard
¼ cup relish
2 ribs celery finely chopped
2 carrots finely chopped
¼ cup red onion finely chopped
½ cup fresh dill
Salt and pepper to taste

Directions:
Drain and rinse the chick peas. Put them in a food processor until chopped but not mushy. Place chick peas in a bowl and add other ingredients.

Banana Bread

Ingredients:
2 cups of flour
1 teaspoon baking soda
½ cup vegan butter
¾ cup brown sugar
5 overripe bananas

Directions:
Mix ingredients in a large bowl and pour into a greased loaf pan. Sprinkle cinnamon and brown sugar on top of the banana bread, and bake in a 350 degree oven for one hour.

Thank You!

I have a heartfelt sense of gratitude for those of you that have read this book. I hope and pray to be of divine service and support to those of you who are looking to walk a path of healing.

The path for healing is different for each person. For some, like me, the transition to veganism will be healing, spiritually uplifting, and joyful. For others, due to blood or body type, the complete transition may be too difficult to support good health. I encourage participation in a more compassionate eating style at whatever level supports your well-being and good health.

Contact Renee if you are interested in learning more about her upcoming unique workshops combining veganism, meditation, cooking, healing, and spirituality.

Email: VeganbyRenee@gmail.com
Website: VeganbyRenee.com
Instagram: Vegan_by_Renee
Facebook: Angel Ren

Made in United States
North Haven, CT
29 May 2022

19649714R00059